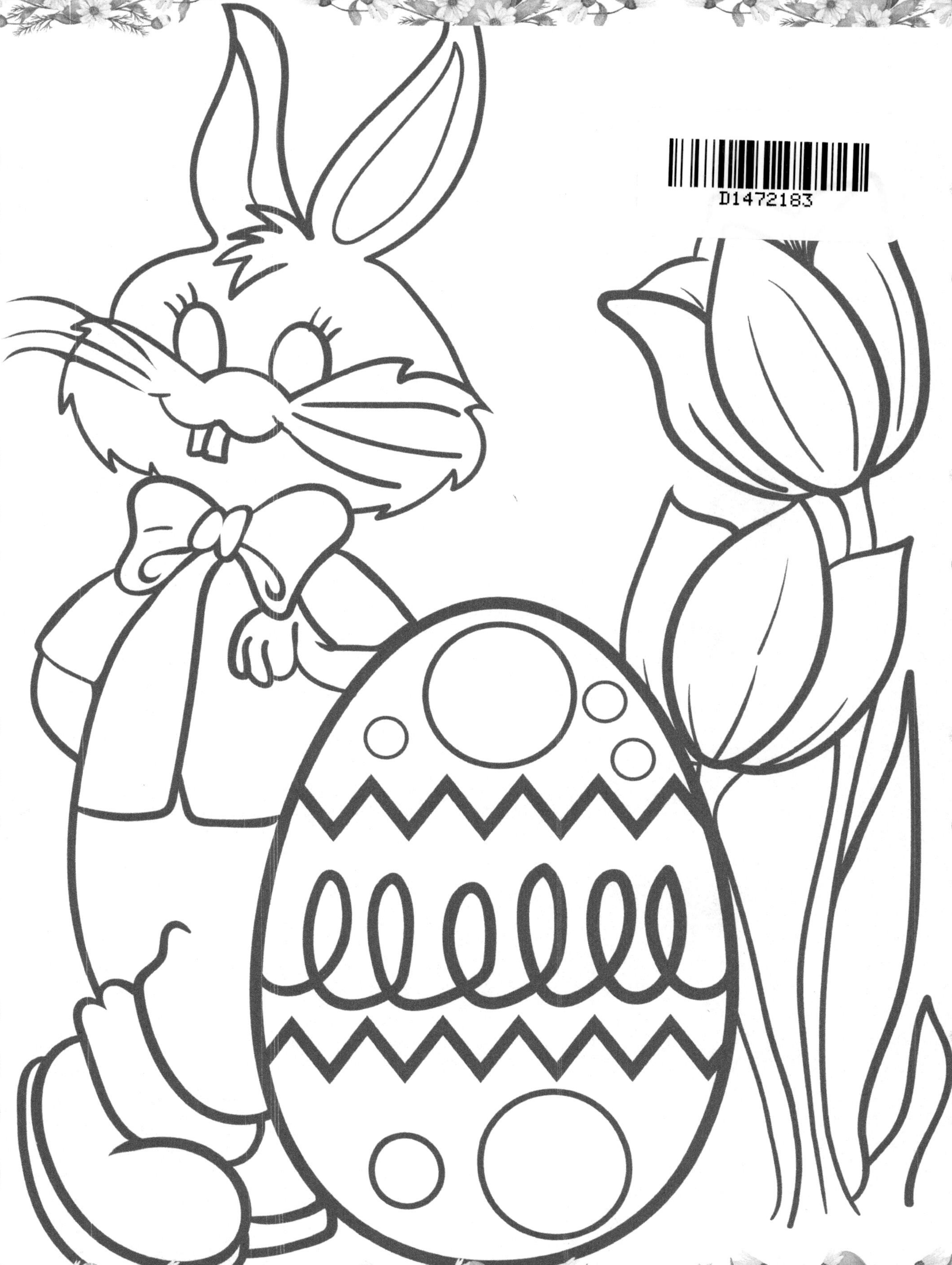

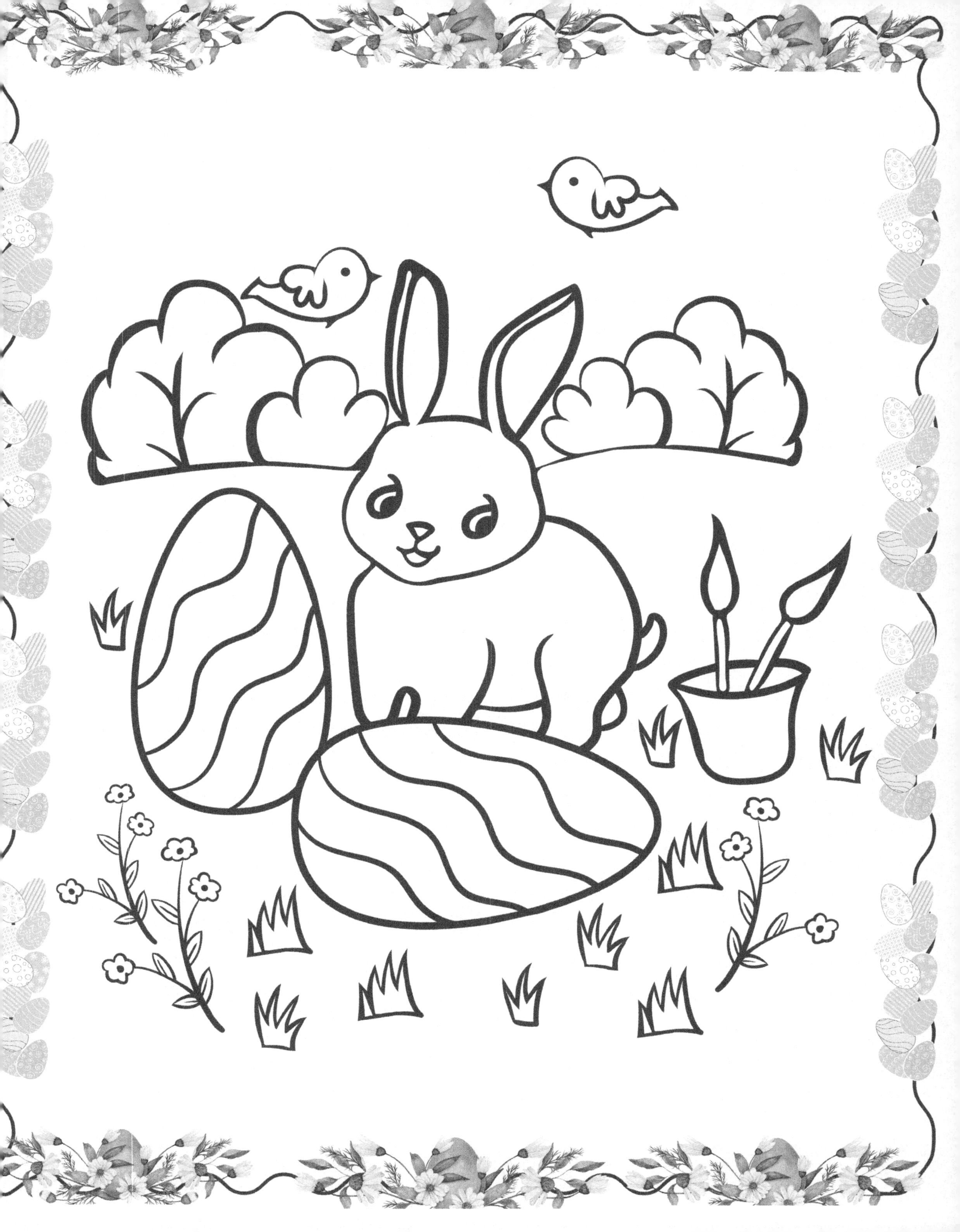

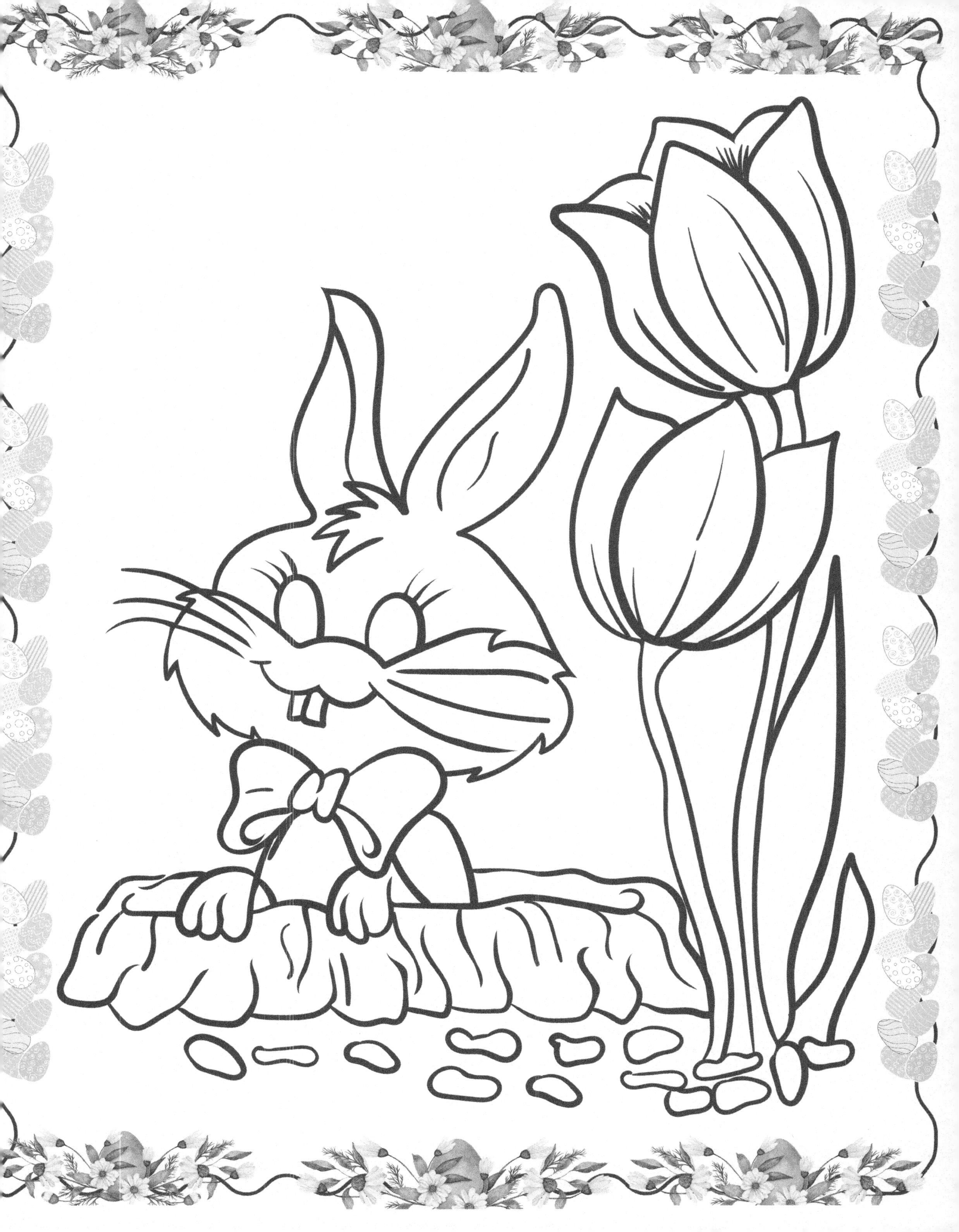

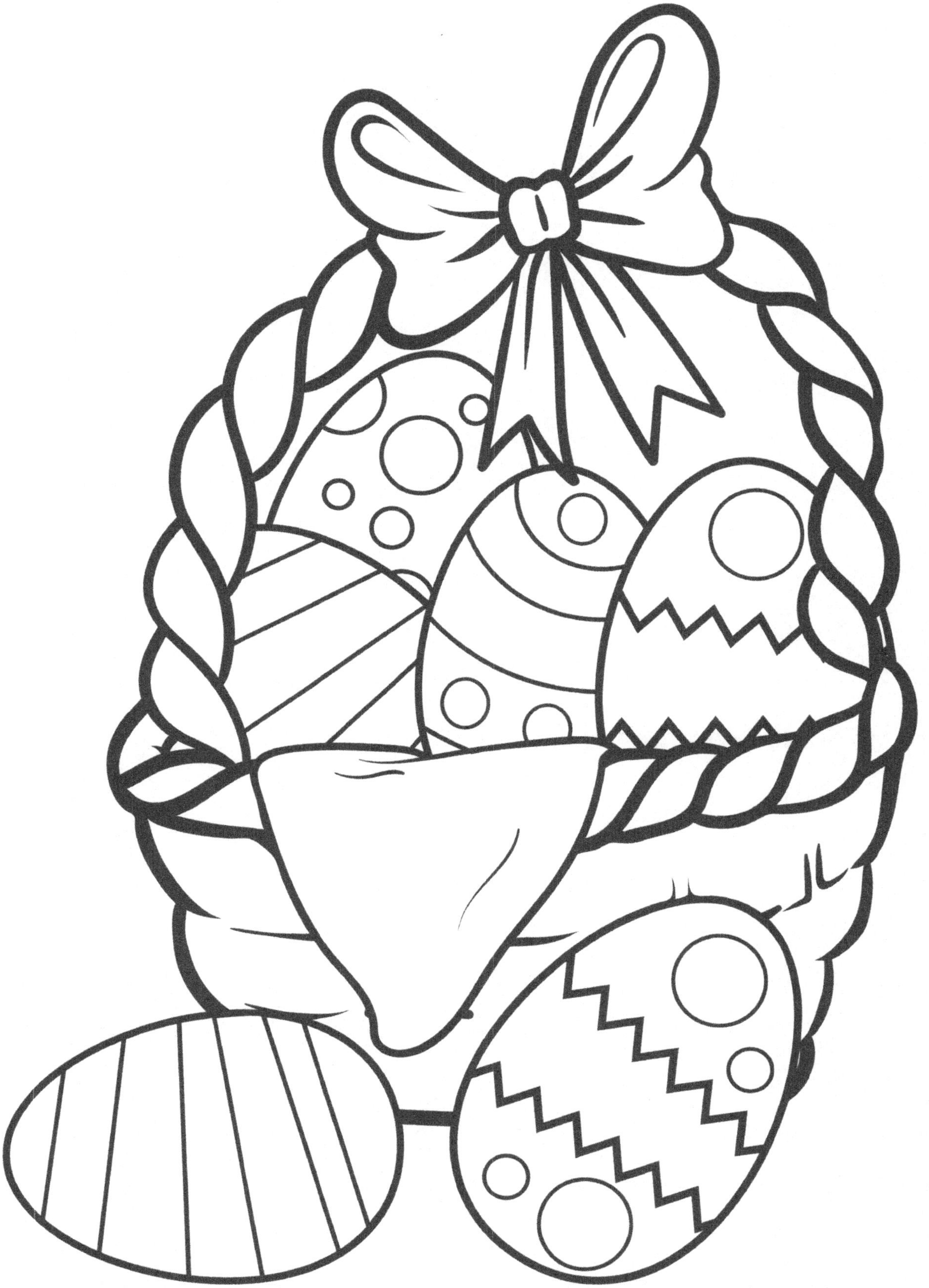

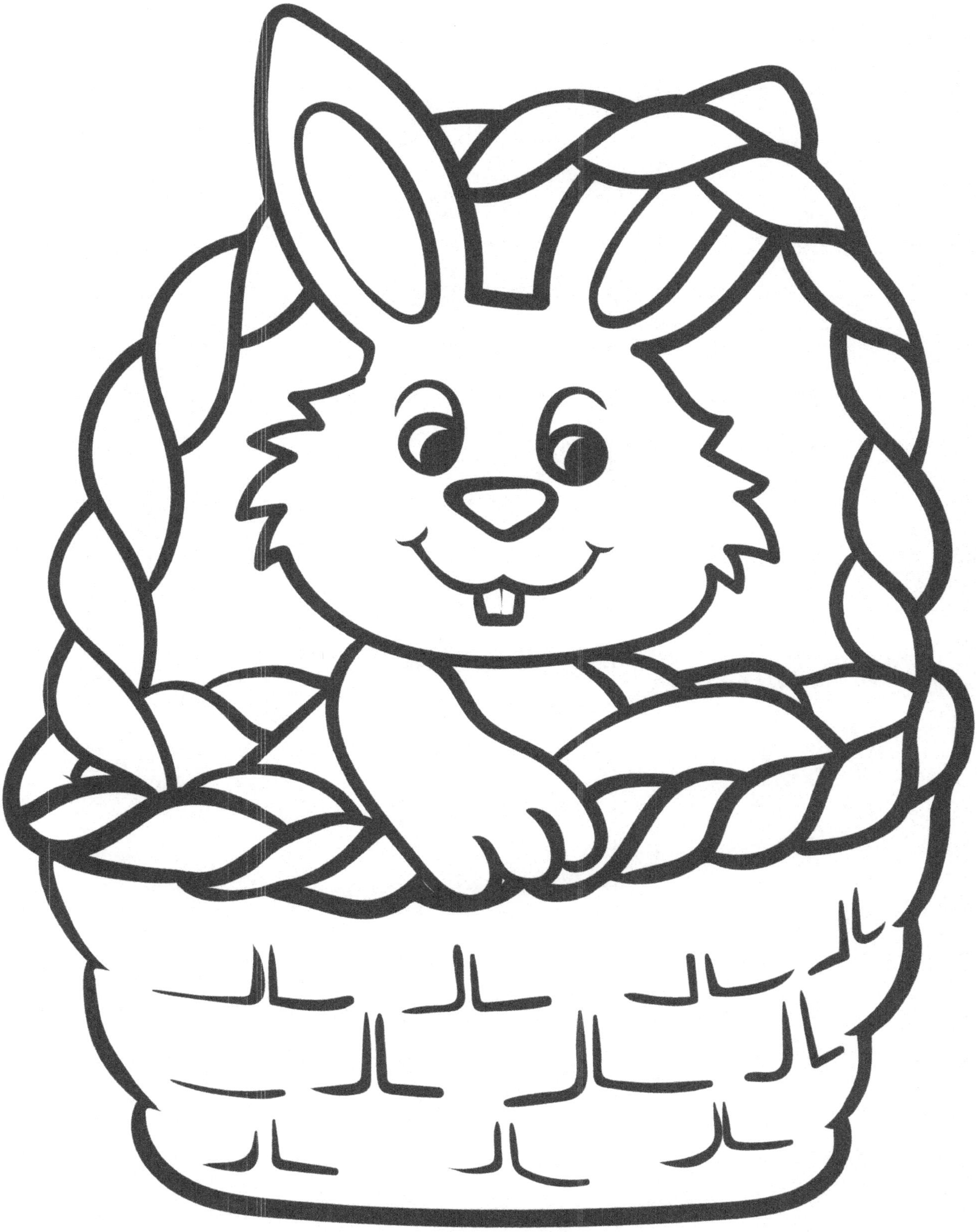

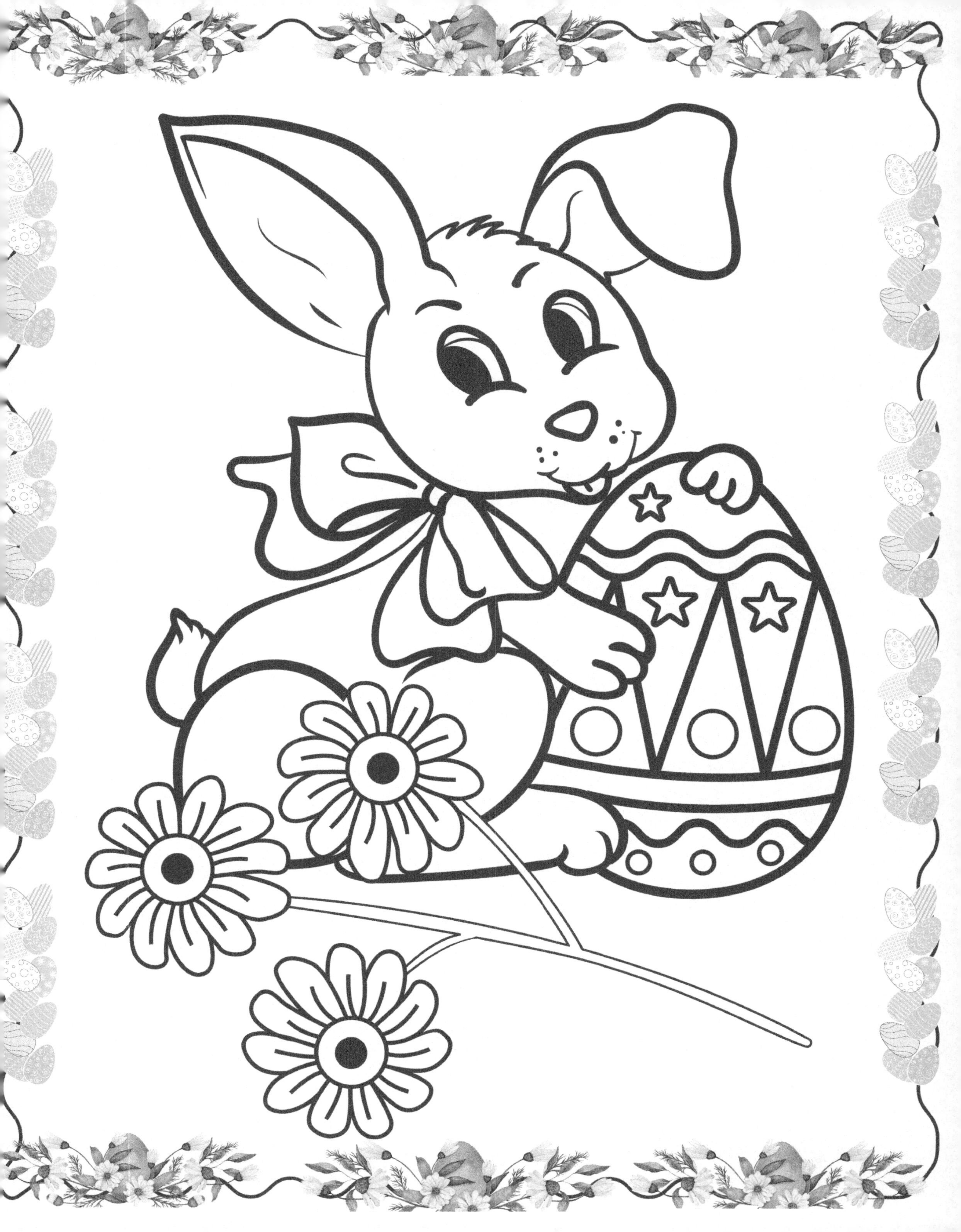

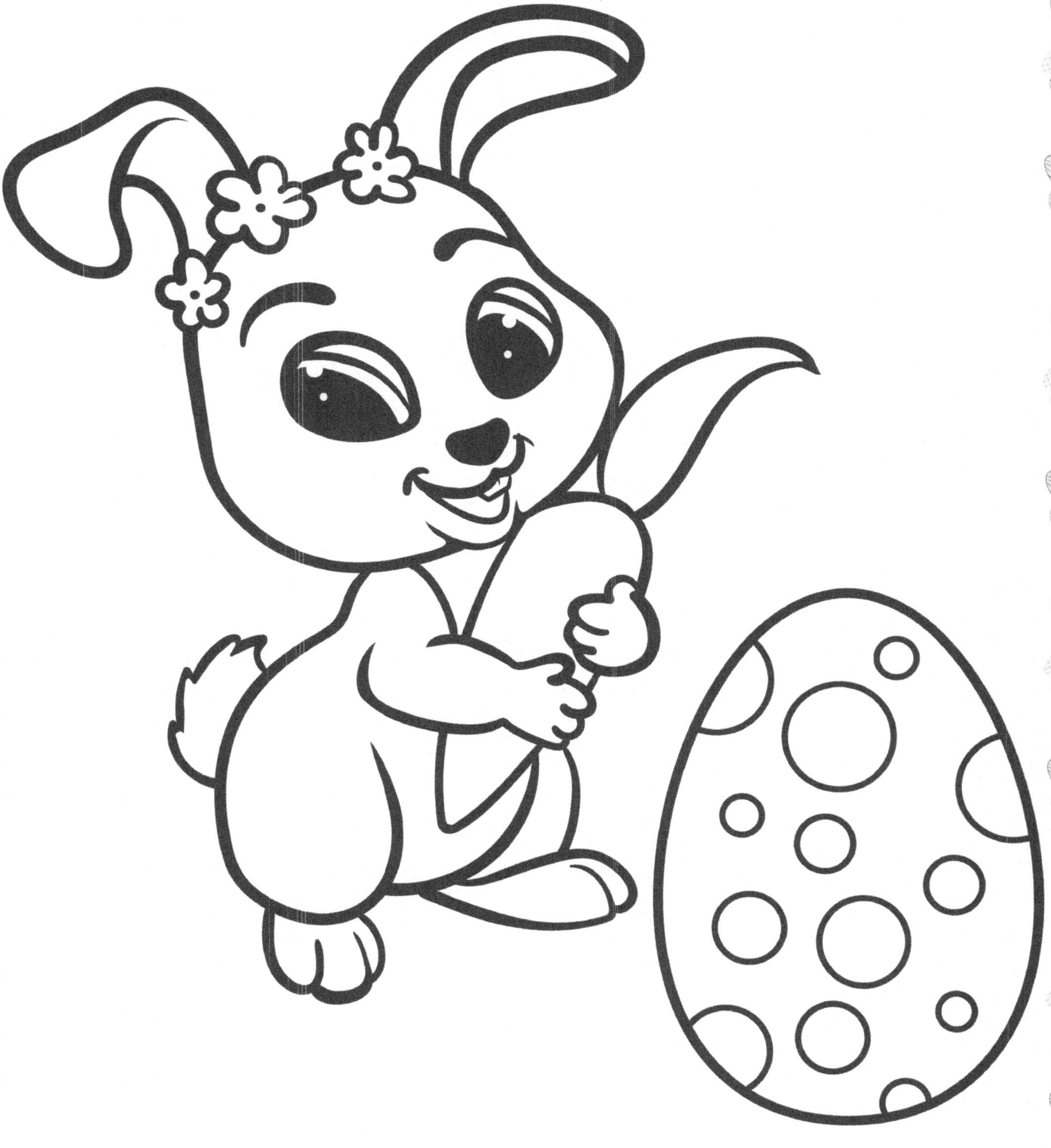

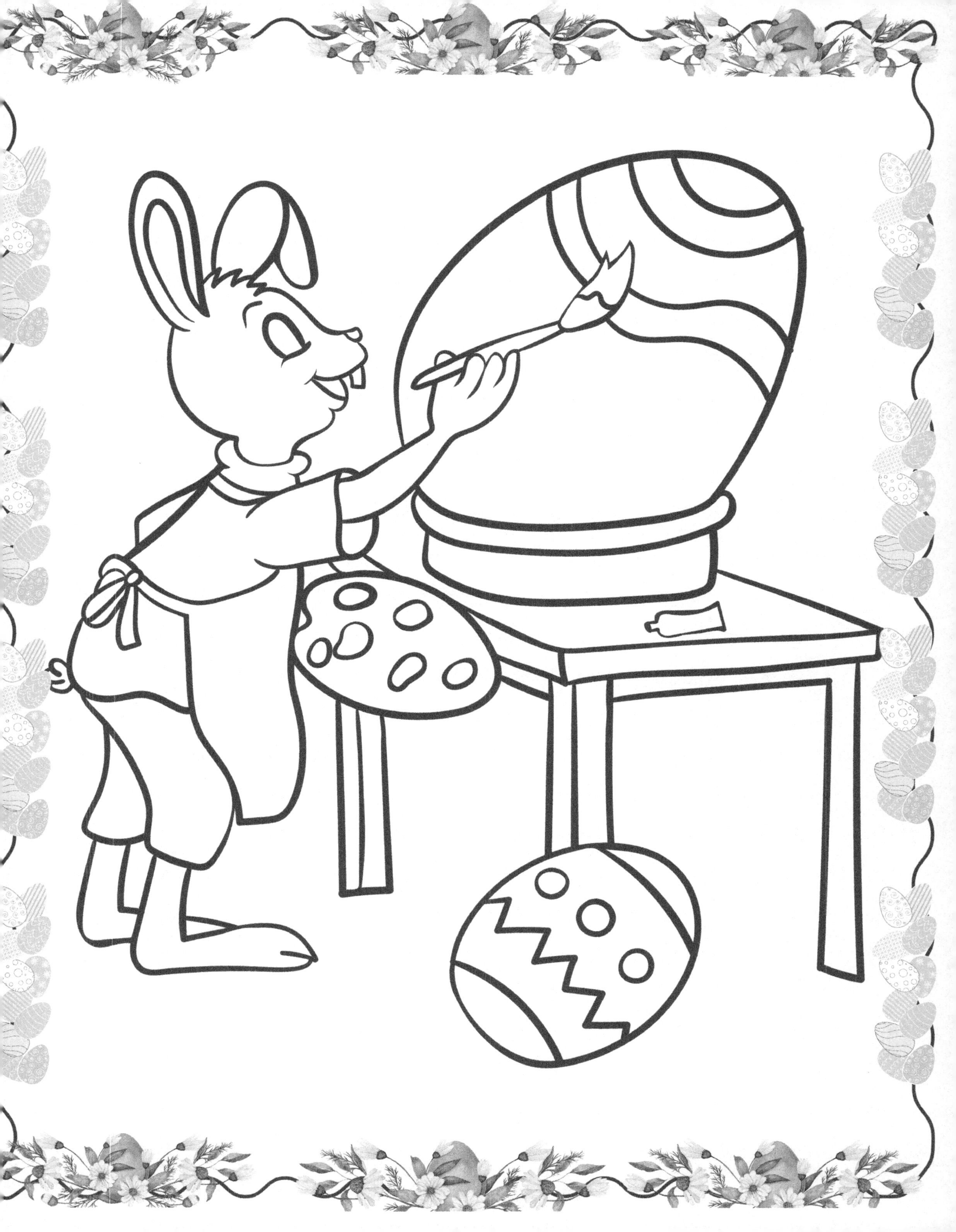

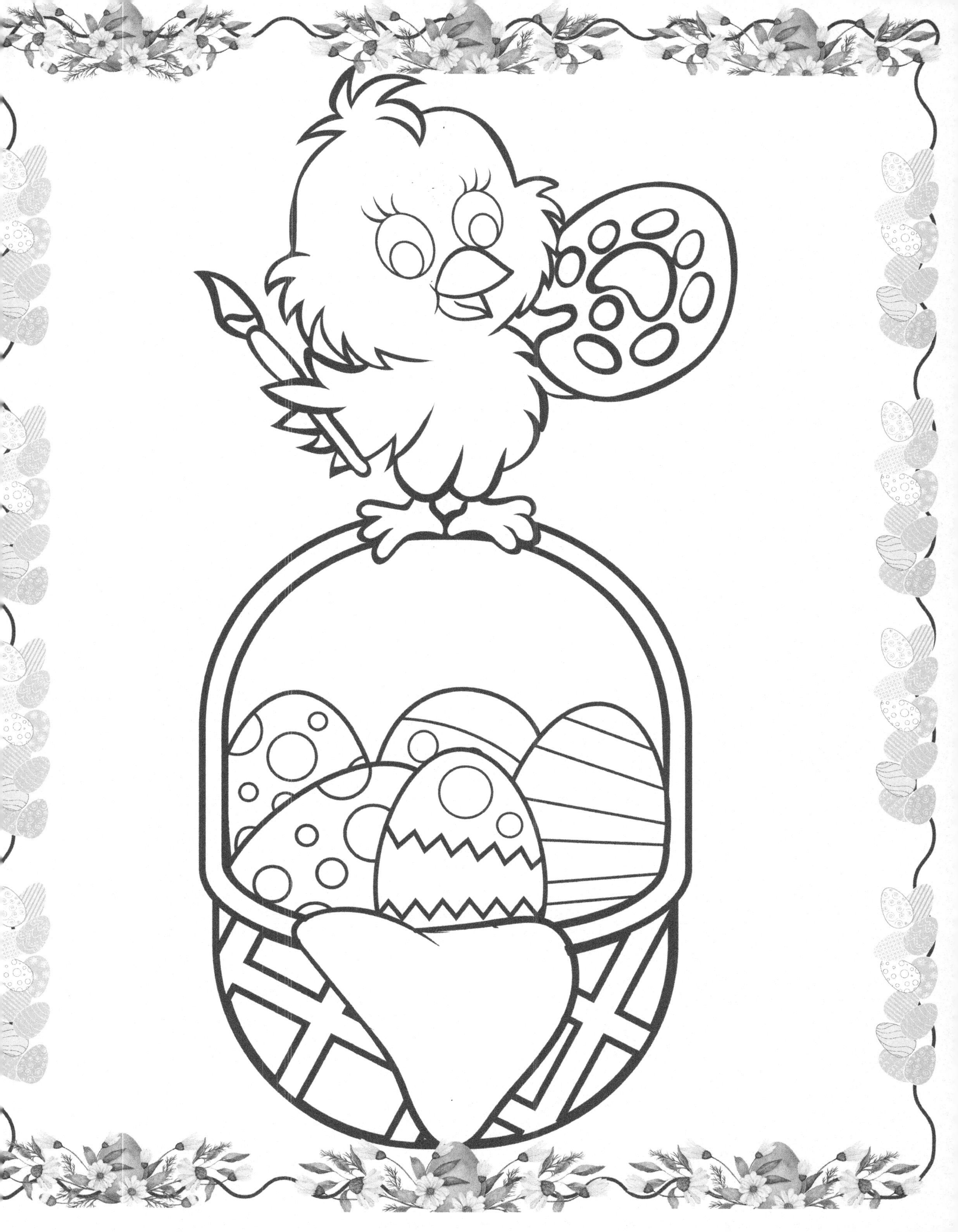

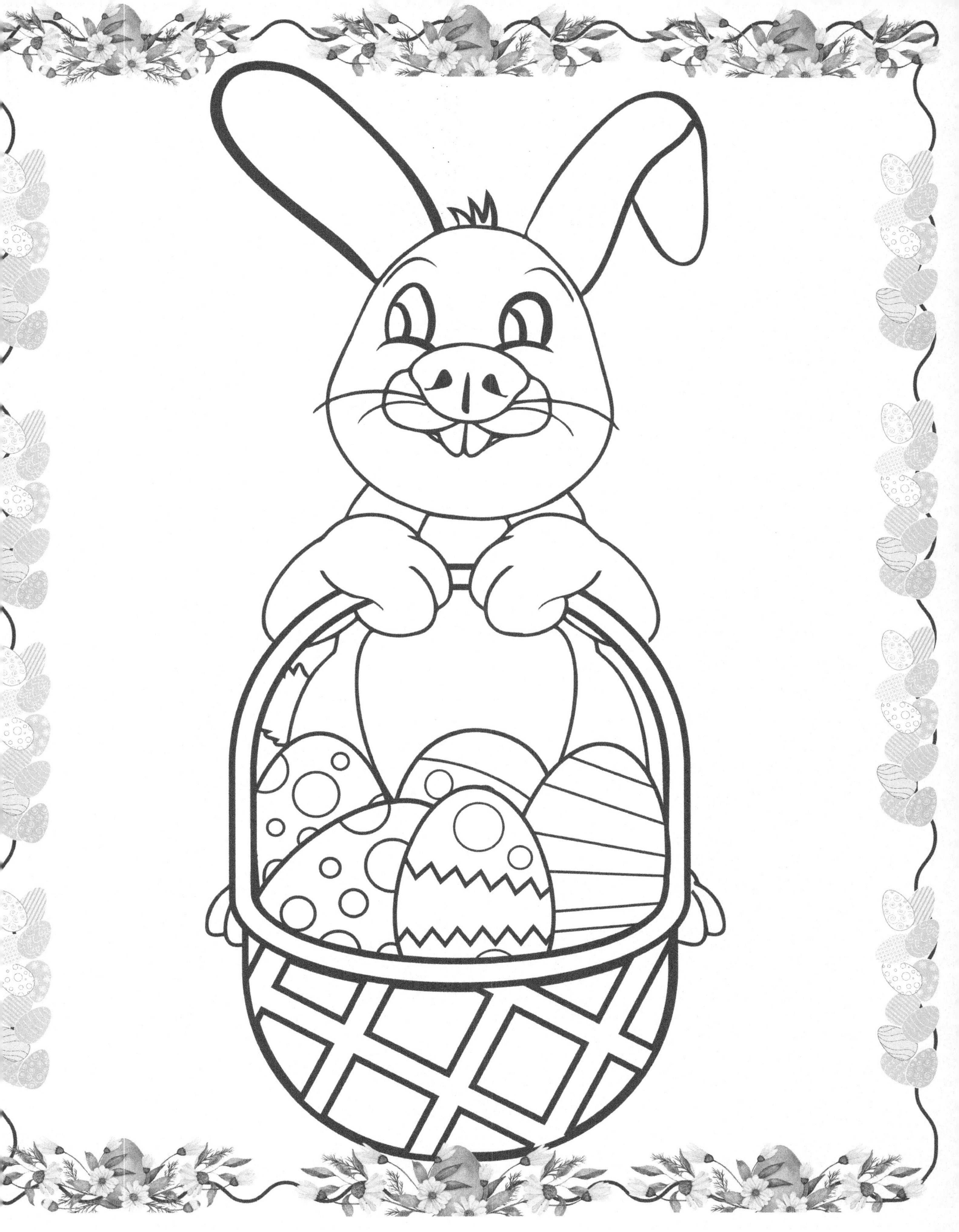

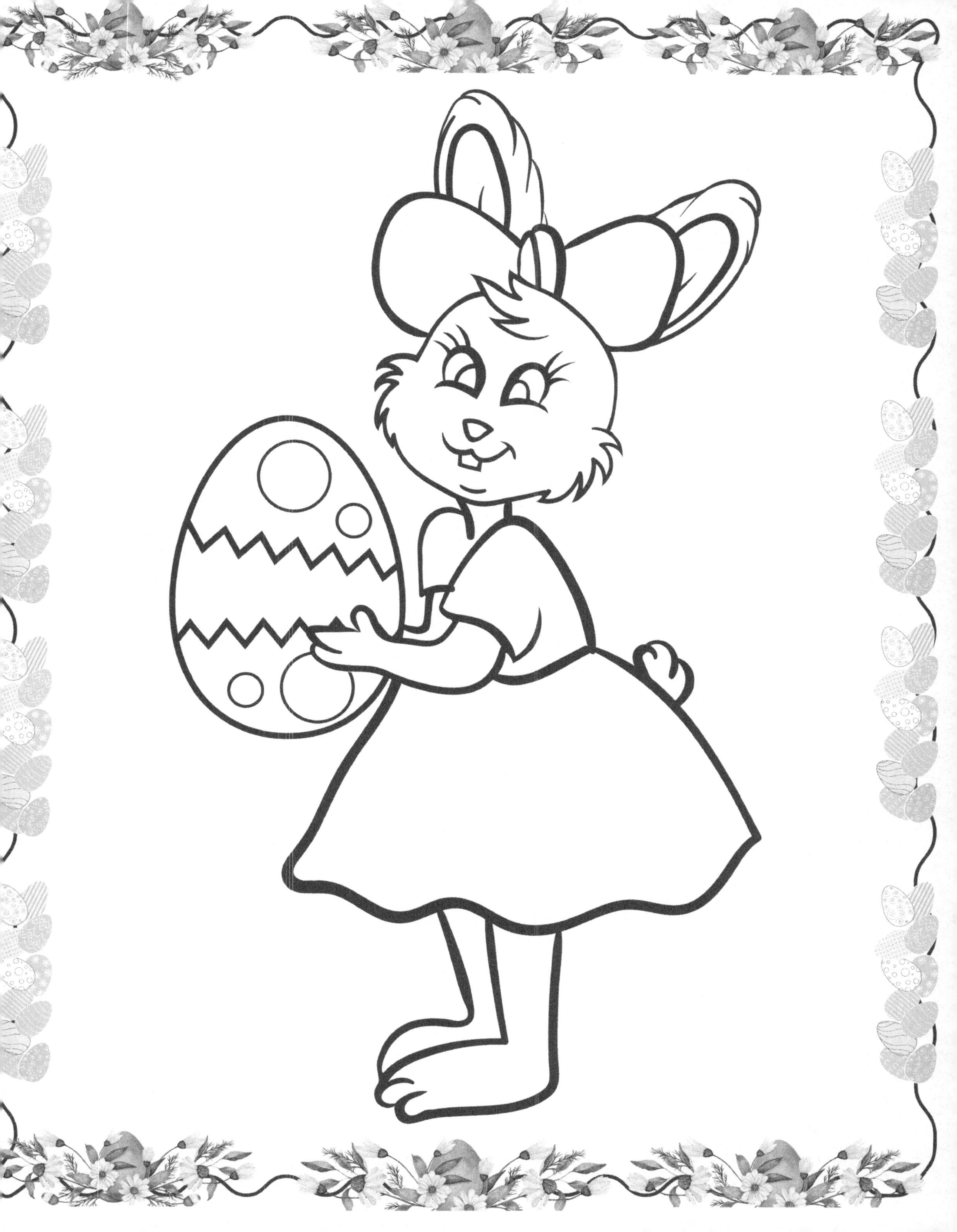

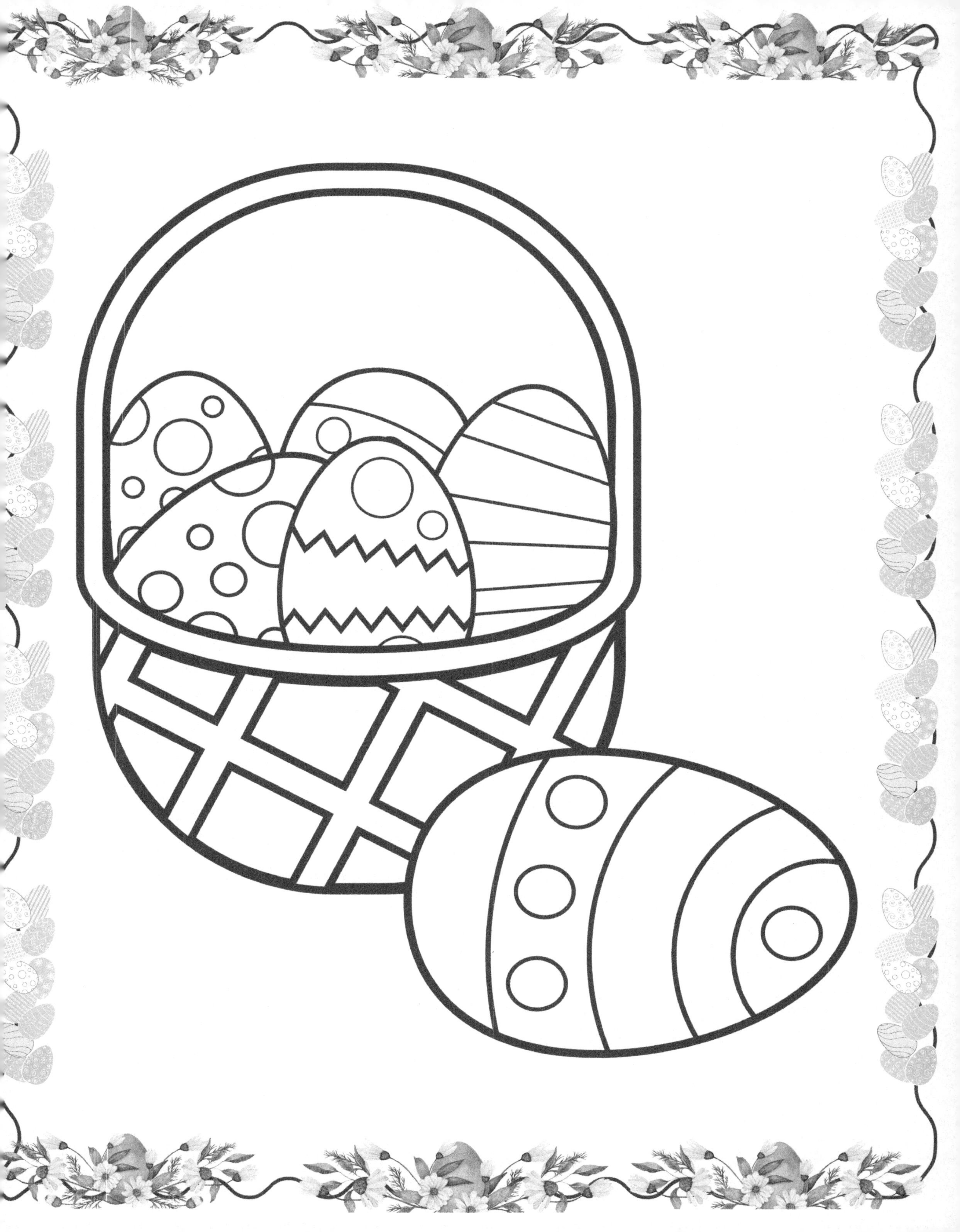

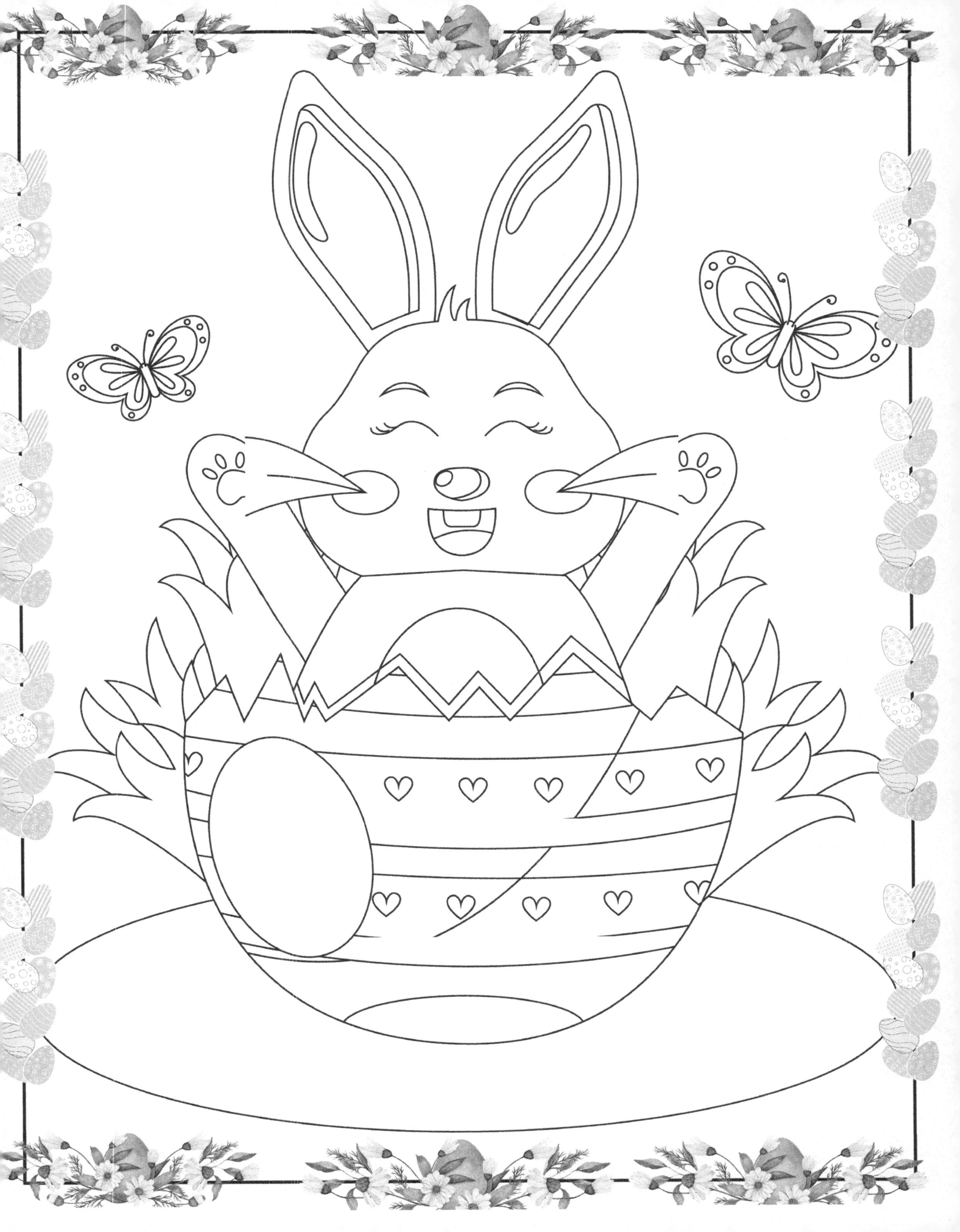

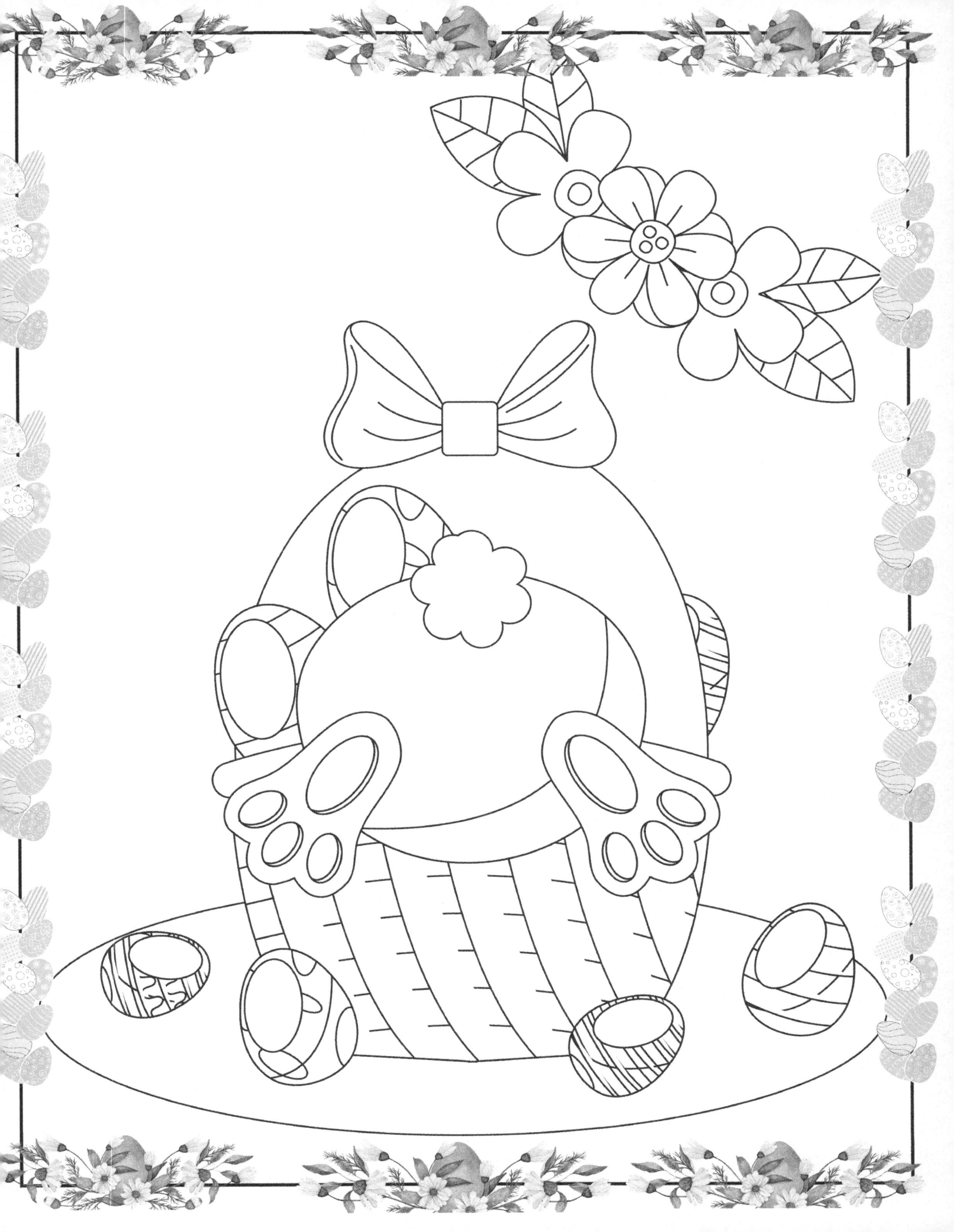

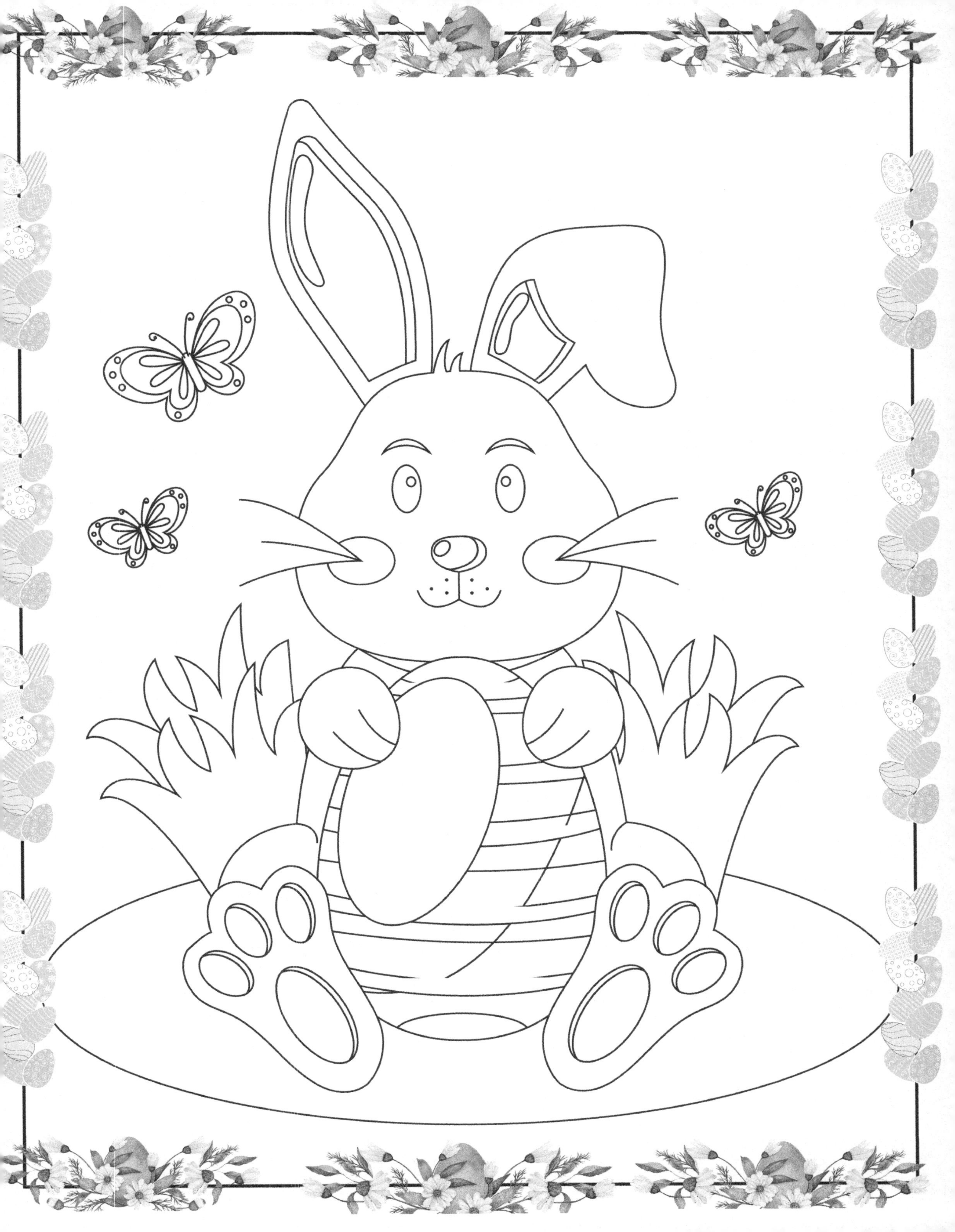

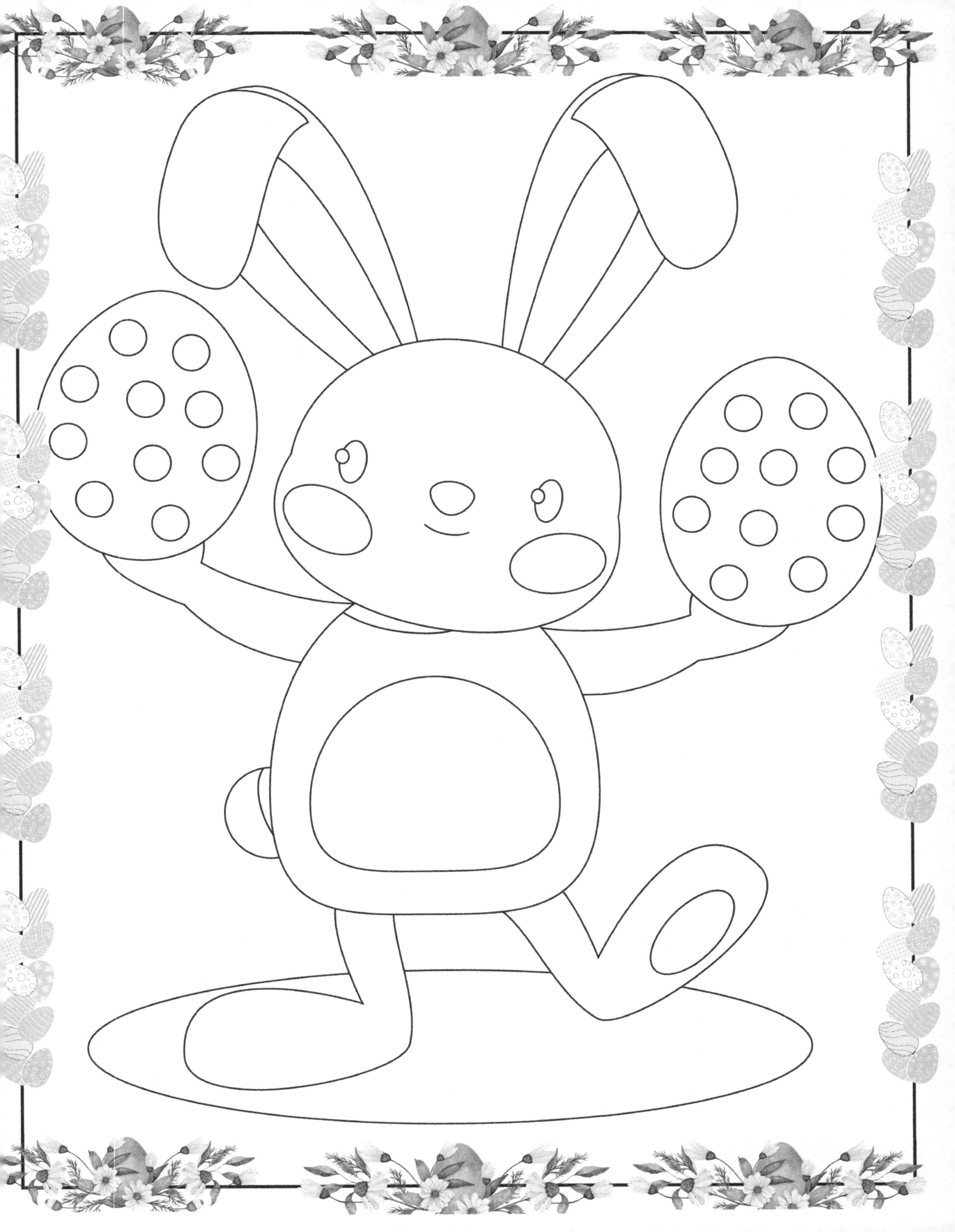

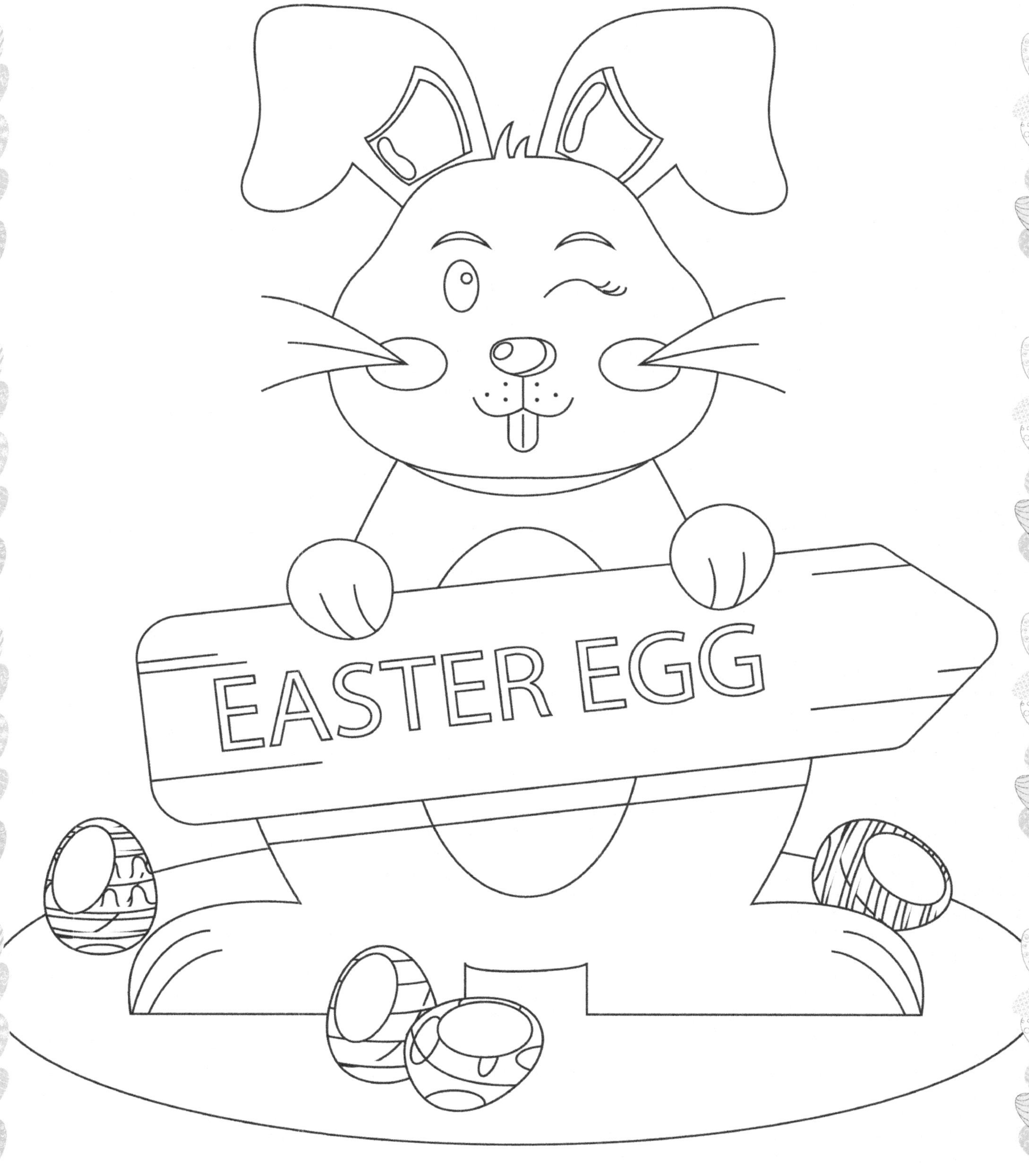
EASTER EGG

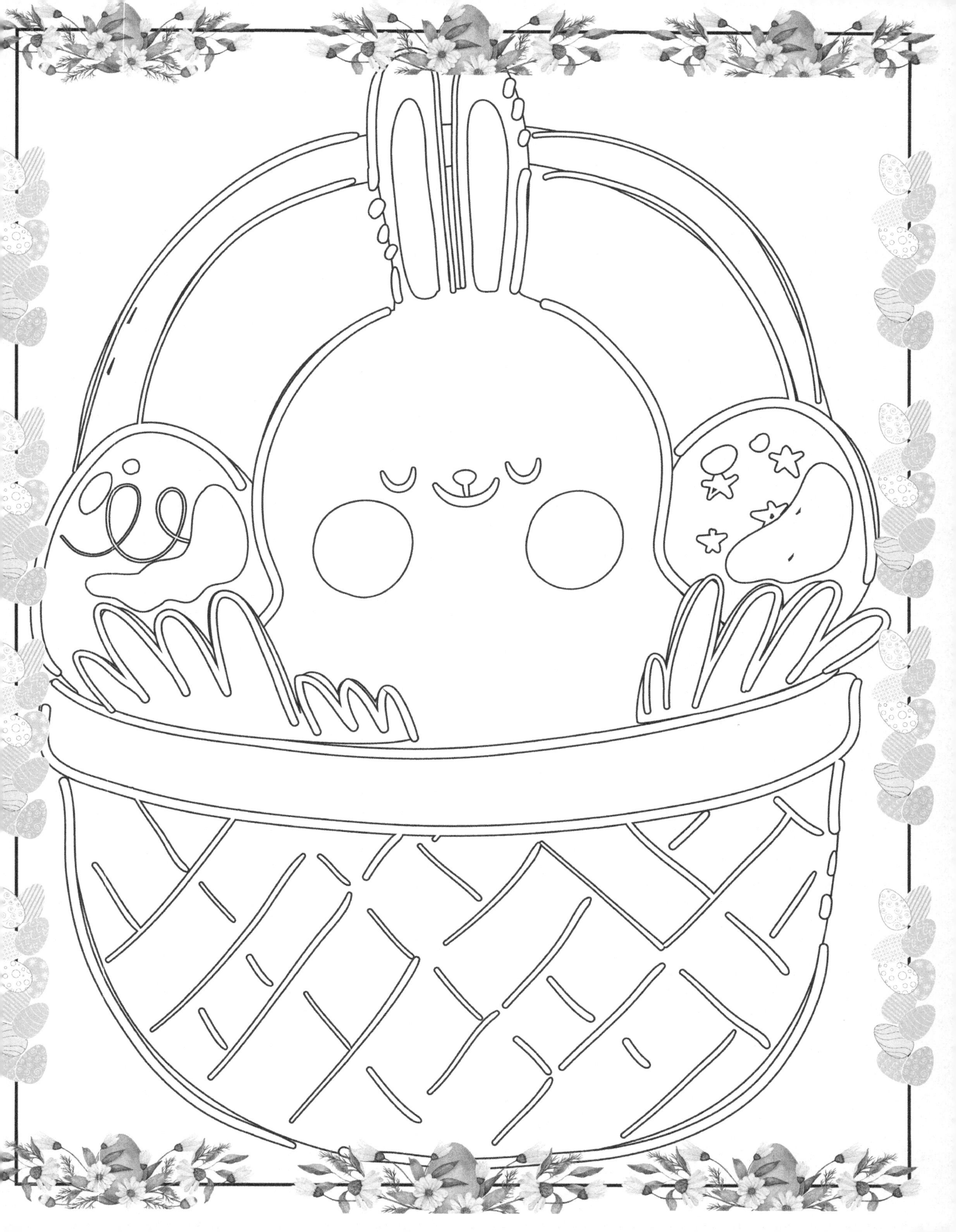

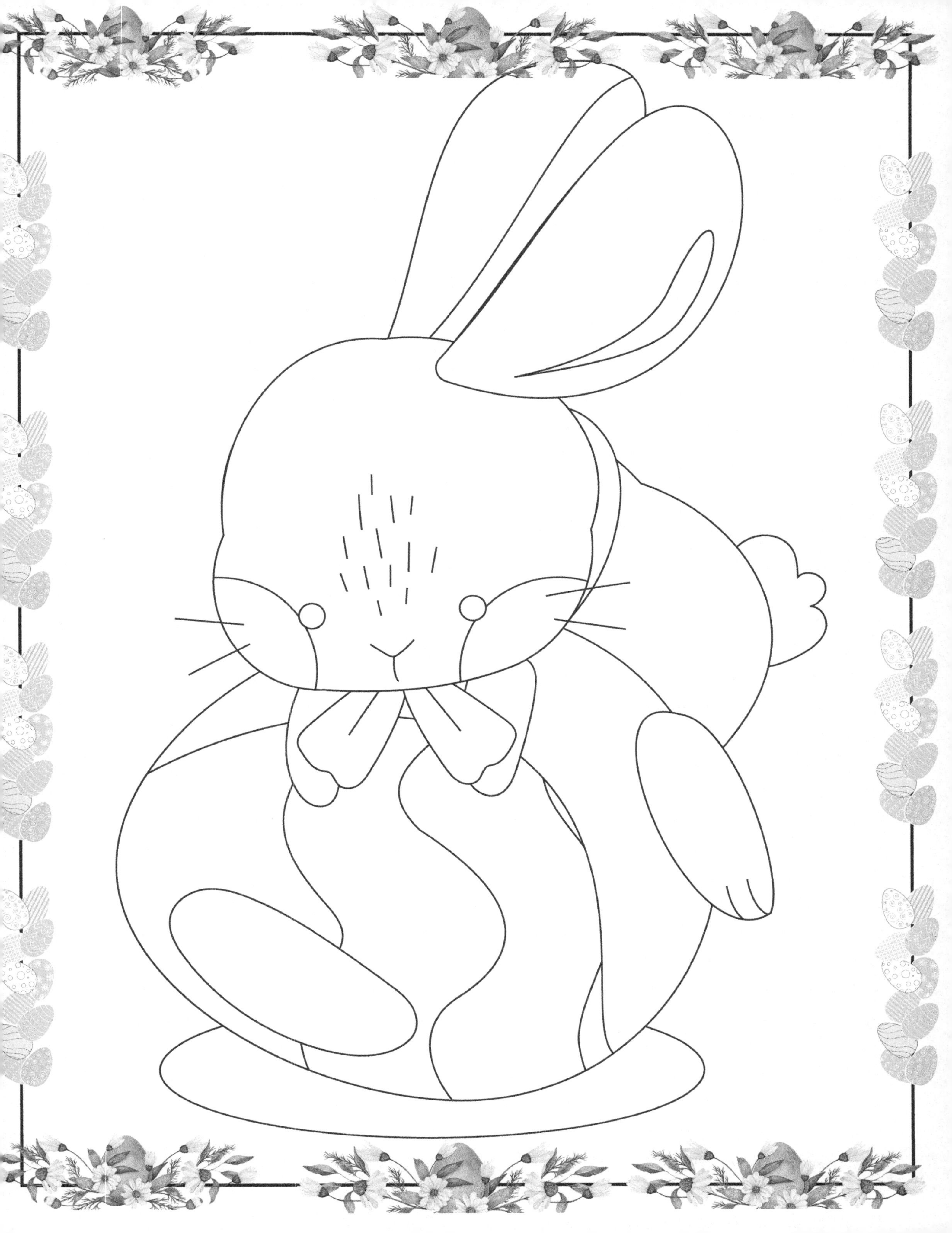

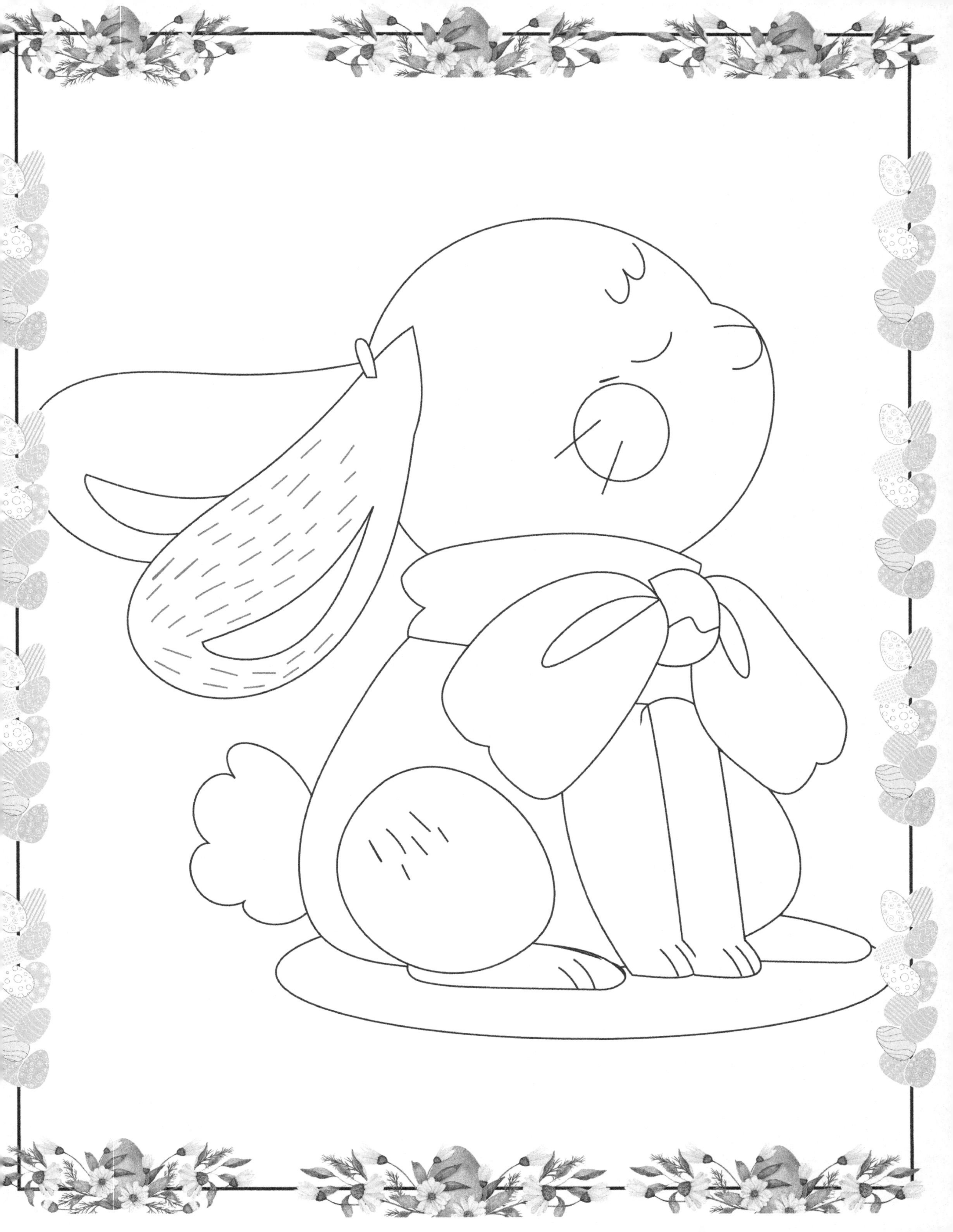

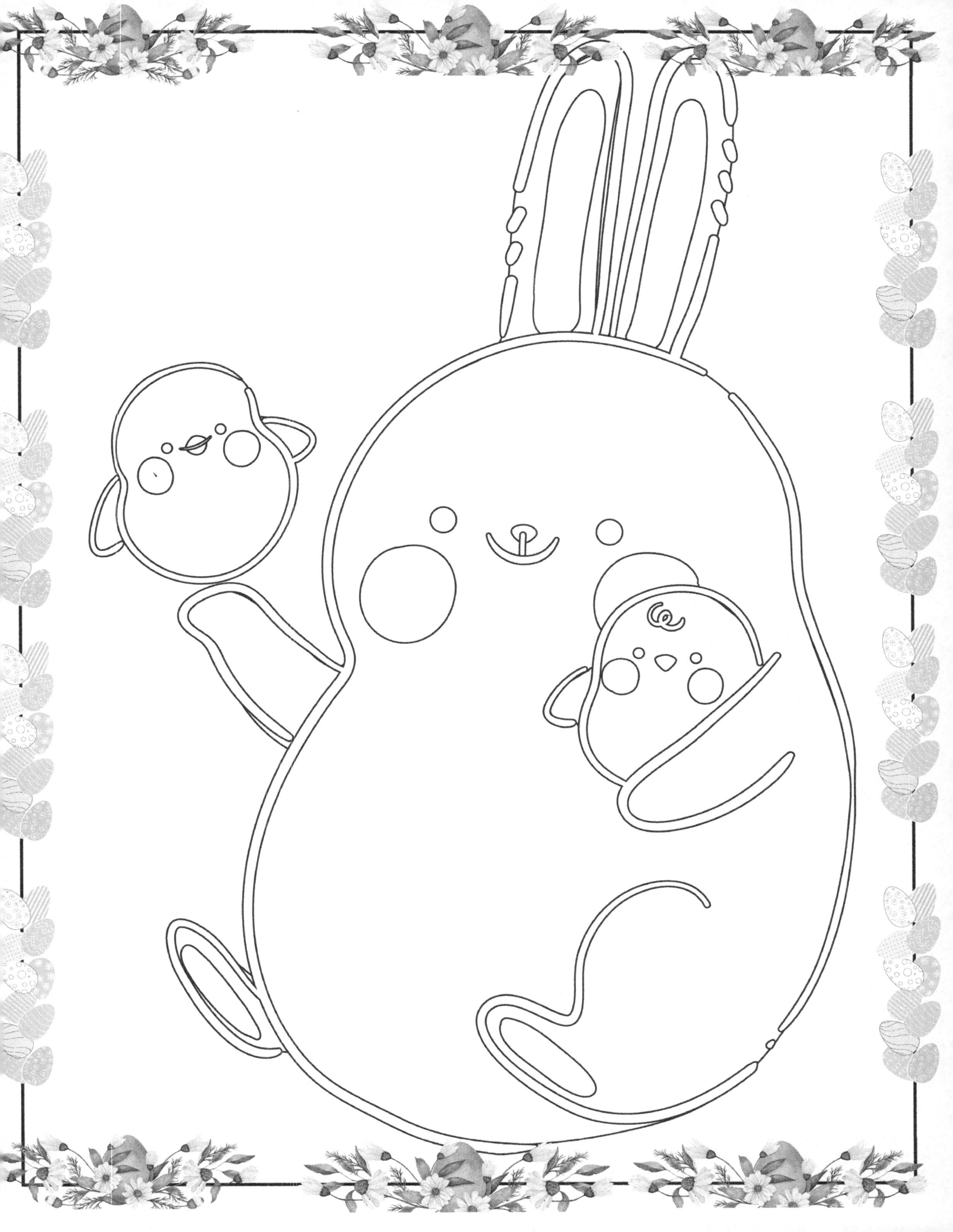

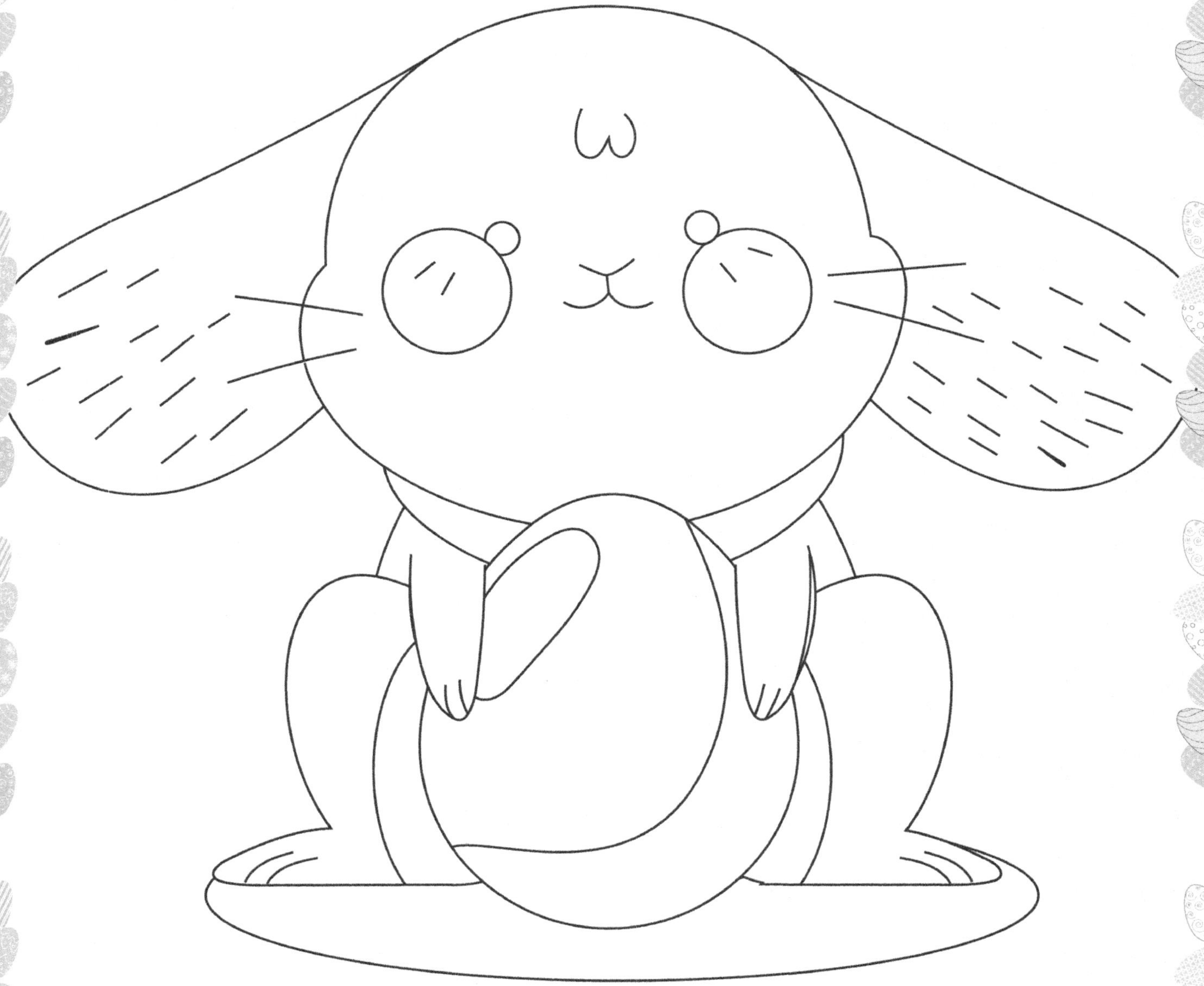

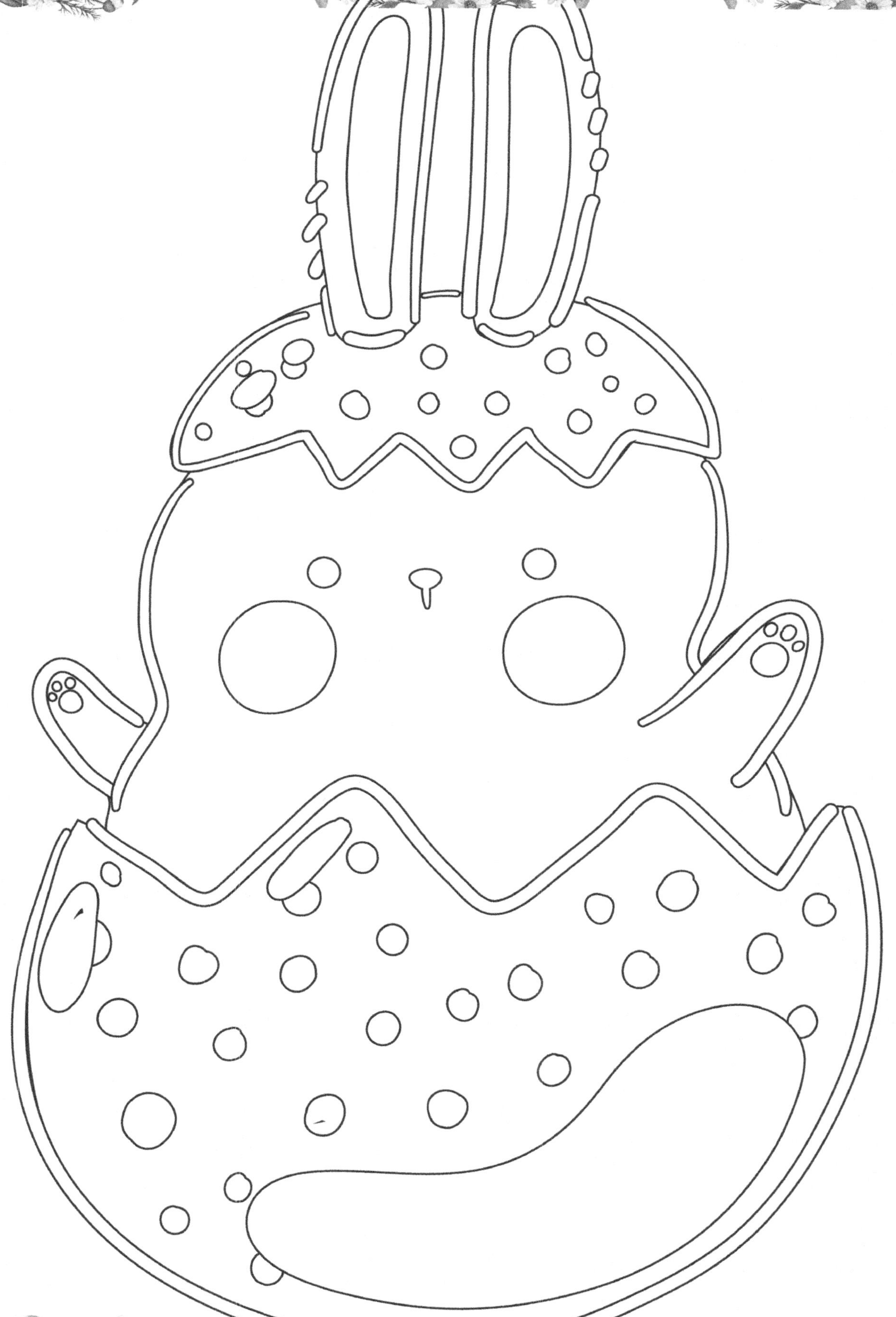

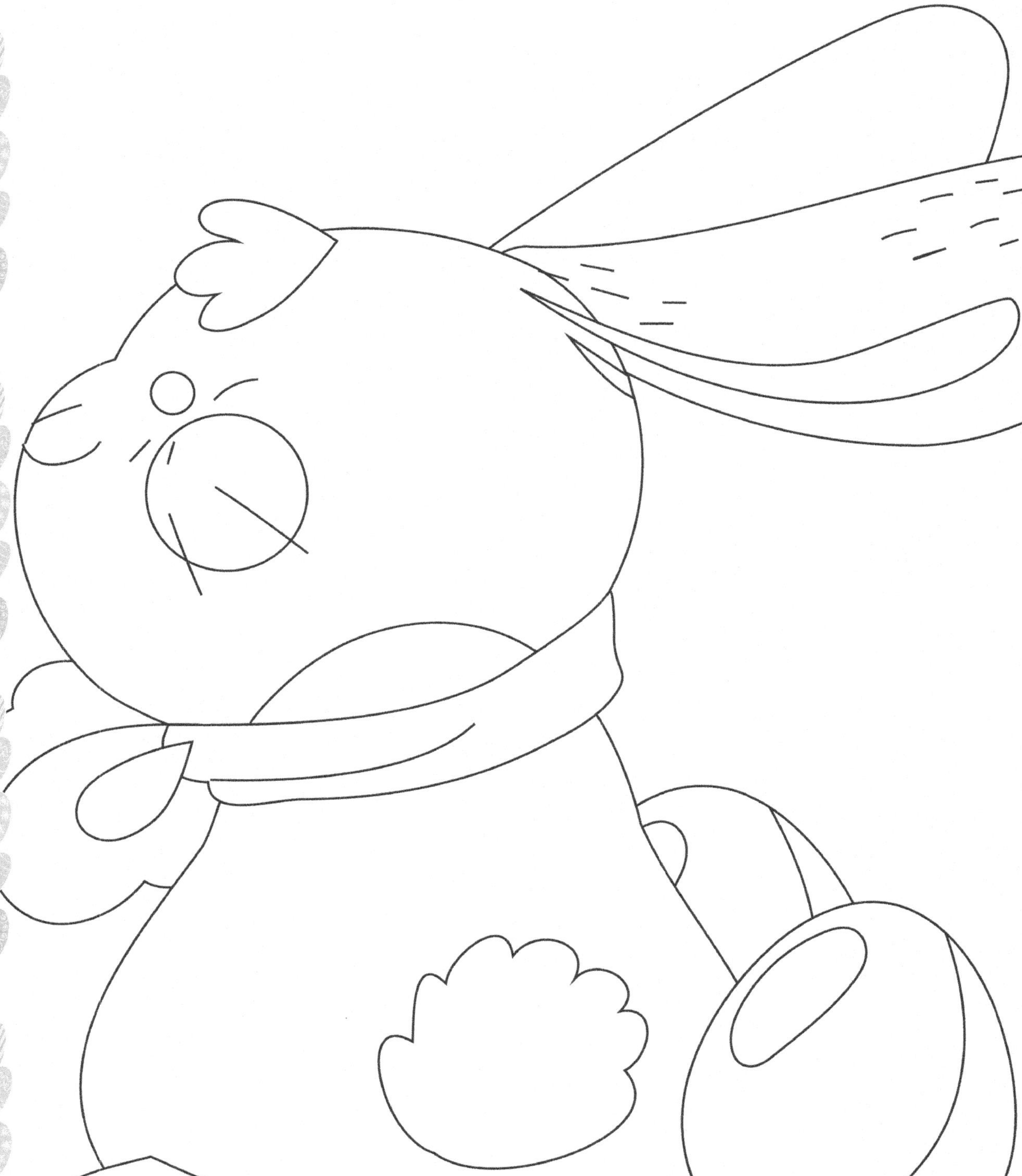

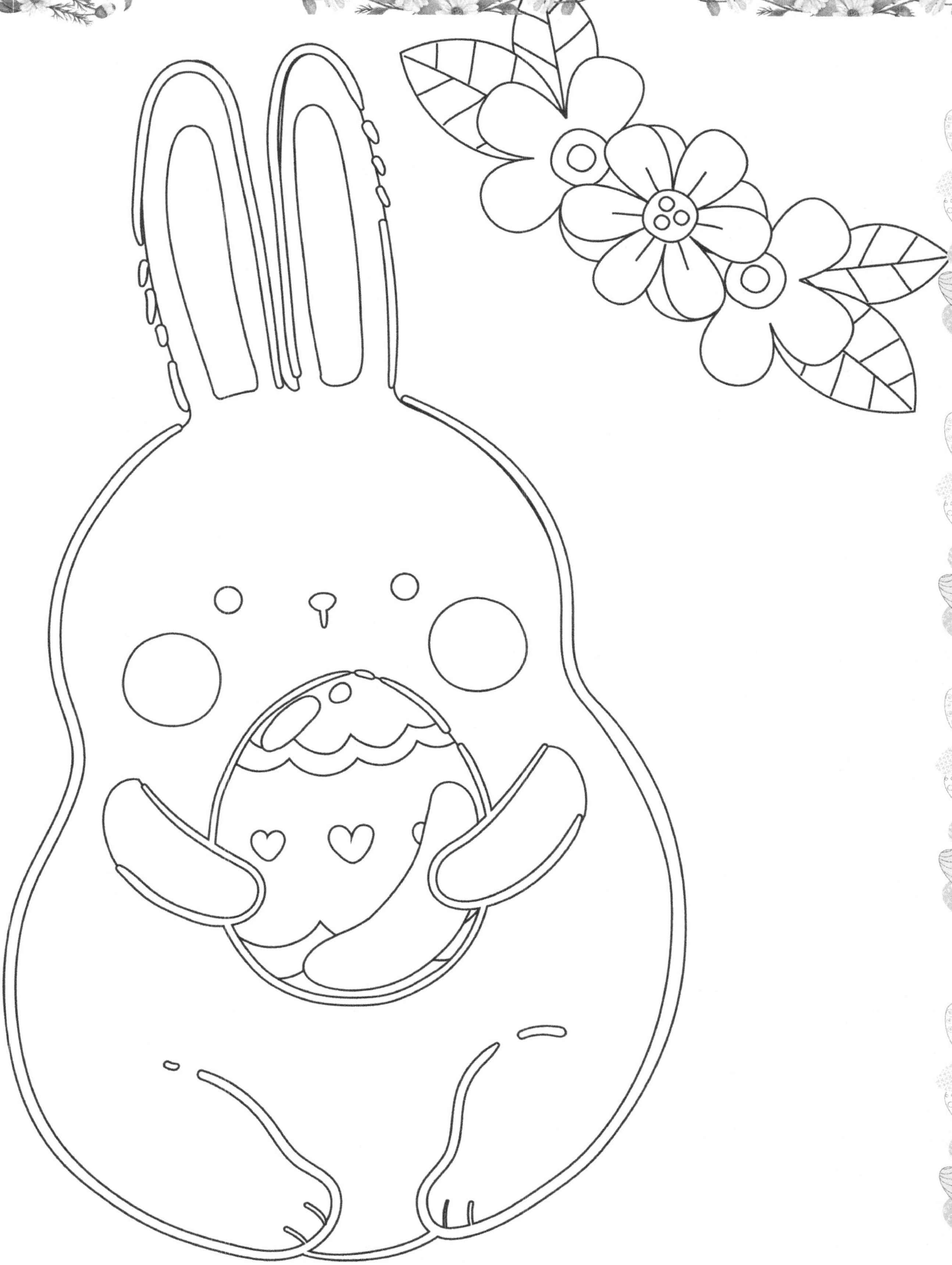

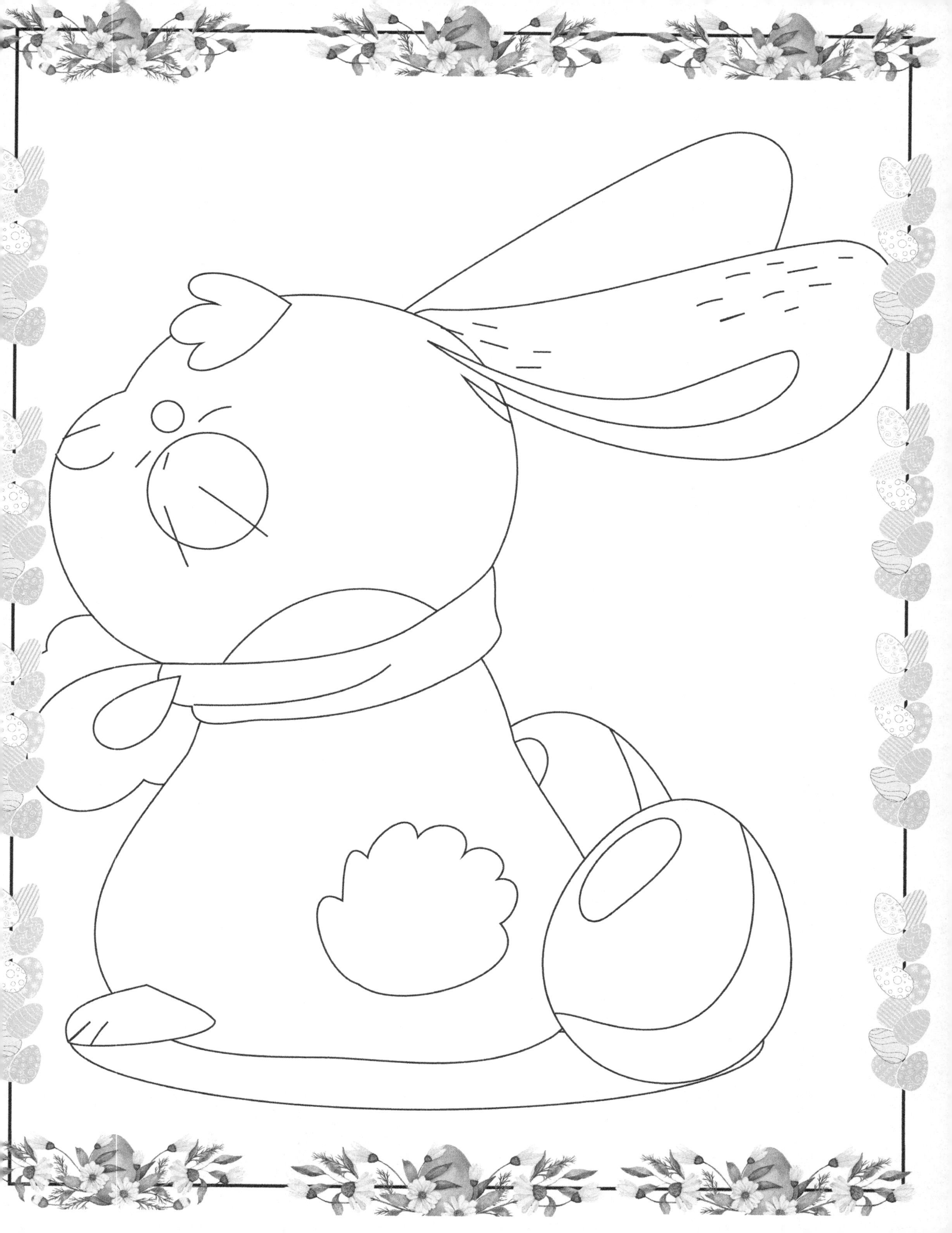

Made in United States
North Haven, CT
07 April 2022

18029505R00030